Under the mackerel sky

To

Adrian

All the best for the future

Steve

22.1.97.

Stephen Potts is Consultant Surgeon
at the Royal Belfast Hospital for Sick Children.
This is his second volume of poems his previous collection is
titled 'Slender Glances'.

All profits from this volume will be donated to the
Royal Belfast Hospital
for Sick Children.

Under the mackerel sky

STEPHEN POTTS

Introduction by
James Simmons

First published by

Pretani Press

1992

78 Abbey Street,

Bangor BT20 4JB

Copyright © Stephen Potts

Introduction © James Simmons

A Nosmada Book

Art & Design Pegasus Design

Printed in Northern Ireland by

The Universities Press, Belfast.

ISBN 0 948868 16 3

Contents

ACKNOWLEDGEMENTS

Northern Bank

GLAZO

Universities Press

Northern Ireland Tourist Board

A special thanks to Jim Egner - Pegasus Design for his help and inspiration which have been invaluable in the production of this book.

INTRODUCTION

My family and I, like so many others, have great reason to be grateful to Stephen Potts. If it was not for him our son Ben would have had a very short life, now he is three and a half, healthy as trout and full of fun intelligence and activity.

I suppose it is not so surprising that a man who is extremely talented in one direction shows ability in many directions. The poets of the 16th and 17th centuries in England were also soldiers, statesmen, historians, and churchmen...Sir Walter Raleigh, John Donne, Edmund Spenser, John Milton etc. Stephen Potts is no easy conventional poet who can turn a few complementary verses, but a writer of subtlety and complexity. He brings his imagination and compassion and quick mind to bear on the mysteries of hospitals and healing as well as more general subjects and his African travels.

Sometimes his mind is too quick for me. I like to be eased into metaphysics narrative and description. Stephen Potts moves straight to what he sees as the essence and point of his subjects, although he can be humerous and humane in his African poems:

Afterwards/In the Spring/I found a letter/From Zachariah.
John Zachariah /has no boots.
Only his black skin/To walk a living/Out of the Earth.
He begs/That this mother/Should not wear him down
That my shoes/ Should come between them.

He is not an easy poet, but he is a challenging one. My blessings on this book. May it sell widely and raise money for a hospital which does so much good work in our community.

JAMES SIMMONS 'The Poets' House', Islandmagee. February 1992.

WHEN BEN WAS ILL IN HOSPITAL

Janice, that time we had to trust machines
to keep Ben breathing. Hope was in plastic lines
that fed him milk and vitamins, tubes that could suck
mucous from his clogged throat. Neither love nor luck
kept Ben among us where he is today,
it was harsh experts and scalpel and X-Ray.
Cutting his flesh, breaking his rib was smart,
detaching his wandering throat from his tiny heart.
We were spectators; but the little shit
was as tough as they were, fighting out the bit
like a warrior, enduring the sore cuts,
surviving, angry and helpless. It took guts
and a sound heart; but the tubes that kept him going,
he tried to tear out recklessly, unknowing:
they forced life on him, more than he could bear.
He preferred death to discomfort, but they held him there.

Your hands and mine could touch his spindly thighs
among the needles, mourn for his bruised eyes.
A long time in that clean well-lighted place
we watched his stubborn head and chubby face,
blue eyes and small hard chin, much like my own,
familiar from father and mirror. I have known
Ben's face for a lifetime. Here he belongs,
with us who stroked his head and sang him songs.

JAMES SIMMONS

To Ruth

PART ONE

THE EARLY MAN

But for the clanking and hissing
Of God's hand
I am dead,
I the early man
Anxious for the world
Have come without a breath.

For my brother
There was nothing only tears.

I am a real consolation
Breathing on invention.
Death complains
Now God has changed.
I, wombed in glass
Am given future
To my past.

GREAT EXPECTATIONS

As I bubble
From the liquor
I have no mouth
Full of the invisible,
Nor of the swish cool crying
I was promised.

My hue is unnatural,
I am blue.
Pulled in
By a sponge
Which puckers;
Sucks at me.

I want a breath to see her,
She who carried me,
Before my breath will hold
And carry me away.

GRANDMOTHER

No longer the painful right hand
No beaming face to celebrate
No certainty in the eyes
That looked inside to test you.

The blowing, heaving, empty sails
That can at best be still
Are the only declaration
That there is perhaps
A wish to be here,
See more, Feel a little ecstasy,
Hear our thoughts across the bed,
Laugh at the quiet paralysis
And remember,
Remember
What to tell Jesus
And fear
His own conviction.

SLIPPED

That was the moment
When my back broke?,
Cracked?,
Chipped?,
Flaked
Imperceptibly
On the films,
And the muscles threw up a soft grey
cloud:
Lightening in the arches!
Stabs of Ante Mortem!?
Post Partum?,
Forgot them,
Melted, started
Into walking,
Running, bending,
Lifting,
Laughing at the thought
Of an ambush in the ruins.

CLEFT

But, for a step
To the left
Or to the right
My palate might be split,
My limb twisted
The time for my departure
Hidden in my chest, belly,
Somewhere in the vault
Mother's, father's, Jesus' fault.

As if a pillory
Could restore the mind of chemistry,
The drunken spell of atoms
Seek revenge in me;
More I
To see their cold perfection falling down
Beneath a soul,
Which I have found
Amongst miscalculation.

But For a breath,
A Hesitance,
The rings
May have been knit
Their spinning kept
In time with other chains
Than give me a mind,
A prayer,
And shadows in my vault;
Only pain have face of fault.

THE DONOR

To be with Gods
To be as God
He dies a God
Taking all his house
To his grave as Pharaoh.

When gone from here
To, atmosphere -
Just soul I fear
And leave my body cast
To kill a suffering as I pass.

And
If spirit is
Just
A fuller kiss
I will have known this.

BIFIDA

His son is rejoicing
In accomplishment
His daughter gasping from her wreckage.

Excellence;
Sufferance:
Collector of the ribbons;
Wishes to escape the normal gaze.
Each achievement made the worse
As pleas for numbness are dispersed.

*I*NSIGHT OF AN OUTLET
(A Bonus of Medical Training)

When I was young
I stood in Smithfield
Or by the Water Office
And struggled with my short trousers
To fill the gutters
Before I burst,
And wondered at the hue of faces
Older than father
There before me
And there when I dribbled and left.
They blew a little
And their eyes filled up at times.
They often swore
Late in the business,
And shook.

Now Time
Has me cutting at the knot
That plugs these sinks:
So, as I stand level
On the tiles of a country town
Where gentlemen and others drain
slowly,
I know
When a squeeze
And running water fails
That little boy who went as quick
They'll beg to flush their tails.

PART TWO

Hibernaculum

I watched a spider walking
In the frost ....
No
Not in, but through or across,
Across his weather bridge,
Behind the felt and boards
Which let the season pass.

Frogs sleep in the mud,
Men have God,
The chrysalis of pages:
Reflections of the few champions.

I saw
Pipistrelles and swallows
Share the dusk
Equally skilled.
The beauty and the invert
Avoiding the colic of defeat.

$\mathcal{I}$SSUE

The sea comes in like a thought,
A ghost of its departure
Bringing memories and the whisper of
a dream.

My breath issues my cloud
Hush,
And somewhere hits the sea;
So,
I have returned from whence I came

CROSSWORDS

Solving riddle after riddle
In the middle of the day
Gives its own special answer
In a very subtle way
But the subtle is a shuttle
And not a true advance
For we all prefer enigma
In the face of ignorance.

Two Beggars

I.   I gave him;
How could you not,
The poor skitter was bones and thread
Dancing between cars.
If he was ten
His hands were a hundred,
Or preserved in the loam
Which counted my money.
For a moment I loved him
And he saw it:
"Some more Sir
For the Mother of Saints Sir
Fifty pennies ... fifty."
He clung to the window
Rehearsed,
Scalded with pain.
Sour froth in his eyes.

II. *We were beautifully led;*
His clubbed fingers spoke
Almost recited with his tongue
Dessicated in the hot eyes.
He seemed to be read - from his speech,
And took me back to ones like him
By the Seine,
Collecting in the evening
Without a thought for Notre Dame.

He turned me,
Every way I moved,
With phrases and soft desperation,
His filth was not there
With his humour;
And it was not there when we fed him,
And he muttered something of faith and
men.

FIELDWORK

On the far hill
They worked all day
They and the red machine
Changing the green,
Weft and warp;
Silently, until late
When the engine thumped
As the wind changed
Bringing them closer,
Even closer than I saw them in the glass-
Then lying in the mottle,
All baled, under the mackerel sky
Roasted in the sun.

ANTS IN THE OAK TREE

In where the sunlight
Cannot hope to find them
Some of them standing,
some walking, some still.
Awaiting the moment
When heaven will find them,
Its wondering light tighten their eyes.
Hunters shall see them:
Who will it be then,
To flavour the palate of some other race.

TWO SHOOTINGS

I.   A watch
Pulsed on the pale wrist
Whose corridors were still
Where breath
And the last will to live
Had run.
Everything was last from the wounds
Helping to instill victory
And cause enough
To kill again.

II.   He may have seen the gap
For a moment. Pulsing,
Then not.
They said he threw petrol bombs
They knew he was shot
Because of the way his clothes seeped
The way he said he was dying,
Then forgot.

THE HEDGEHOG
& THE SOLDIER.

Thorned, soft belly, armoured,
unarmed:
Helmet, truncheon,weapons and
trained:
Caught on the highway, on unknown
land:
At war on the street, his home next at
hand:
Frozen by headlamps, caught up in
fear:
Struckdown in the conflict, blood from
his ear:
Rolls up tightly holds his spines
out.
Rolls up tightly, 'Help' is all he
shouts.
Killed and rekilled by the passing
cars.
Murdered by riot which gives special
powers,
The Hedgehog and Soldier are both
under flowers.

CAUSUS BELLI

Unleashed
They would race blindly on the mud
Toward the sea
Toward the land
On the mud.
It might be said; that there was only
heaven and mud
When the tide was out.

But why hold them by the neck?
Out here
Quick dogs have no need to be quick
Even the geese
Will outrun them.

Its a lean figure that
Walks the black and brindle hound
And dare not let him go
For they hate retrievers
Who know their way around
Who know their limitations
And live on lost and found.

It was other dogs I saw
Who stole the writhing shadow
And would not let him go
For they lived in the mud
Called Holy Ground
And could not cope
With lost and found.

CALIDRIS *(Sandpiper)*

On the grey
Interface
Fresh from its unveiling
The waders
Stab and scramble
For the unarmed members
Abandoned by the tide.

So precise
Not frantic
Like the diggers of lug;
Backs breaking
Ears slapped
By mud giving,
Shovel cutting.

To be close
Only for the sake of watching
Is all but impossible,
As Calidris flocks
And leaves the mud pocked
With foot marks and bill stabs.
Breathe out of sequence and they're gone,
But they stay for the luggers
As if diggers are diggers
And only lower forms are writhing
In this light.

NUN AT MULLAGHAMORE

Good Sister,
I can see you love the tide upon your
feet;
Have you chanced to meet the world?

Does the freezing surf hold more for you
than me?
Surely, rare, this be for you.

Sister,
Have you kept your gifts
Under that uneasy cape
To serve our God who gave them,
And fed your open senses
Rather, than they, you?
Although, with all the children's love
your heart be swelled,
Should you not have held, your child?

Schools

I need a few words
To take with me
To give life to the things which haunt me
To lean on heavily,
When I fail to understand.
I need them
To disguise,
To build, to destroy, to taint the truths
which I employ,
To find reason for what I've read
And have not said.

$\mathcal{A}$ MAN AND HIS DOG.

Not his
To have his head held
By a friend
His shoulder gripped
Answering the needs of solitude.

Not his
To have his lank hair swept
By a hand
Unfavoured
Bowing to his favour.

His only
To wipe the sleeve, turn the collar
On a rag
Passed on
For him to hang upon,

His only
To hold, to grip and slap
To be enjoyed
Crumbling
In the hound's dark eye.

PRIVATE ROOMS

Plunging
Turning the right hand
Forming the perfect dome
Passing grey water from the grid
Up stands the mop
Its warm wooden limb
Draining out the wash.

Satisfying
Purifying his Private Rooms
Deifying: the smell of warm soap
Passing off the tile
With a twist
Round table legs and chairs
Teaching disinfecting
Correcting
Accepting People are defecting
Both to his left and right
Suspecting each entry out of sight
Behind those public doors:
Pencils, knives,
Bravely score
Their wisdom on his walls and floors.

GHOST

There is light upon my face
That no longer exists;
That is
Its place
Its time
Where it began.

Stars are listening to me
On this end of summer
That have
Already
Ceased
In their own way.

And the light that sweeps
A warning off the rock
Has lit
My face,
Now travels out
Past night and day.

Am I a ghost already
Seen here and there
That is
In some place
Some Time
Where I began.

J AM NOT DEAF

I am not deaf
I am not blind:
What sight
Or sound
Will leave behind.?

MASS EXTINCTIONS

When the Great Rocks come
We will simply be no more.

That
Sun of Suns
Companion Sun
 Blow out our mark
Like Haley's feeble breath a million
times.

So sad
For angels
Fooling poor Giotto,
Putting down what Bethlehem foretold:
Gabriel and Michael
Forgetting what they know
To tell the greatest story
Ever told.

MECHANICAL DIGGER

Clear air
Frozen hill
Quiet black
To dignify the open earth,
As we have need
When they leave us.

And a man with a spade
Turned the earth in upon the wood,
As fire would light the long ship hull,
Bringing things together
At the end.

Quiet black
Today
Is by yellow overrun:
Scooping metal
Puffing heart
Dumps and levels
Pressing down on all thats said;
Grinding
Till our prayers have fled.

DEAR JACK

Beautiful Jack
Is subtlety black
His smart grey cap
Off the nape of his neck,
So bold is the blue of his eye.

When he's single that is
Jack Daw is like this,
But when he's in flock
He's of quite different stock
Charring the wind as he flies.

Like the Rook
He is spooked by his suit.
Although really much better
He is let down by his sweater
When around with the Upper Class Sky.

Open your mouth Son of Man
Say,
"I am that I am"
Raise the head off your neck!
Ah!
I was wrong to have thought it Dear Jack.

*V*ACANT LOT.

I'm a perfect circle.
I'm a perfect square.
I'm a common rubber
And I've rubbed you out,
So there !

Instantly Winston

With a saw
I made a window in a egg, - Truly.
 And found somites
Curl upon a head.
Little blocks of future
Changing with the hour
Yolk suckers
Shaping yellow, somehow.

This is a Laboratory story.

Then the sparrow noise
From the window sill
Seemed in, not out!
The oven knocked!
Sound unlocked
And out a Black Chicken walked.!

By some neglect? A holiday?
He hatched by some mistake,
Left the pure white cell
Intending to partake
In the journey round the egg.
Black, he was.
So instantly - Winston.

He was upset!
Had escaped the experiment
But sinned against science
With no right to be blessed
For in an hour he was mad
With no - feathers to touch
With no - sense of the Clutch.

'Cause he'd known about air
Before hatching,
About wetness and breath
But, no incubator death;
No light at thirty seven
No life before heaven.

He banged his head hard, whistled,
mad whistle
And was brought to a farm by the dusk
We thought Winston would have made
friends with others;
But at breakfast was stiff as a crust.

FANCY

She sat to play,
and let me watch her fingers,
Split the flax,
tying my whims into curls
That blessed blue eyes.
(They would flight into the shadows,
Lit upon the wall
given breath by sun on set,
then back to me
with some new life to kiss, and say to me
"We live")
Tongues flicker till dumb,
Caressed into silence
by the touch of an eye,
And hands that wander
on timorous fingers, inviting in fear,
with power,
a moment or a timeless tie between us.

To TOUCH.

Can I touch the life in quiet water?
Can I touch
Where mist Is almost morning dew ?
See when ebb tide turns
To flow ?
Can I touch you ?

Gossips

Slip me gossips from your corner
Where your heart
Does part your lips,

Hold me fixéd in the dark,
In the depth
Of what you've said,

Pass here, slender
Hopes in glances,
Threading pains
Long pulled asunder.

Break in gentle
To my corner,
Wish my wish,
From you upon me.

*F*URTHER ON

Wherever
There are rushing sounds
Talking
Or silence that bursts the heart
With vision
Give me your anger
Should it be all you have to give.

Let the wind carry you
The stillness becalm you
The light be our scribe
And the darkness give us peace.

This is a good path
We two are the same in what we have.

PART THREE

THE KILIMANJARO
SEQUENCE

*M*ARANGU GATE
(Picking the Team)

Sea of Black
Talking Black
Deep pool of Africa
Shifting on the ground
Below us,
Throw us out
Its tattered men
Its smiling men and boys
And runs into a stream
Uphill.

PORTERS

Freddies feet
Are oozing red and yellow
Burning on the stone
Knotting back
And smiling face
At war
Beneath the baggage.

John Mafala
Has no teeth
A goat
A cow
And no tin walls at home.
He asked for sixty dollars
But we knew the truth
And gave him proper due.

Seraphim
Wants my shoes
John Zachariah
Wants to write.

So: I gave them watches
And bathed young
Freddies feet
So he can trail
The others up to Kibo
When I,m home.

EATING AT HOROMBO

Semolina
Shot with jam

Hot potatoes
Cut in half

Cold sweet juices
Stick like blood

Boiling tea
As strong as God

Does me good

Along with all my medicines,
That keep out flies
Keep bowels dry
Ensure my sleep
Ensure my feet
Will hold me up
Tomorrow.

*L*AST WATER.

Till now
I had no thought
Of the last breath
But now it comes
Above Mawenzi
With only one half of the life
I had by the sea.

And beyond here
None of the water
I have sipped from the rain,
Only the mud of animals
To fill the bottle up.

My Red sea is sand
I have my stick
And no Sinai.
I am not pursued
Only pulled
By the God of the mountain.

Gone the last water
Come the last breath
If it can.

DINING AT KIBO : HYPOREXIA.

Layer upon layer of glucose
Wrapped up in brown woolly tea
Two pairs of cake in my stomach
High Altitude tabs make us free
To make streams like the snow
Our water doth go
Escaping with breath in the flow.

Five jumpers of humbug
And old furry hat
Fill us up with more sugar
We are instantly fat
A biscuit and gum
Some brandy not rum
Skins next to creeping homespun.

From lightweight to leather
Jaws strain on the nuts
Grind relentless on raisins
And scrape out the ruts.
Steps on volcano
Taste of the moonglow
Tonight and tomorrow
I'm sure,I don't know.

SUMMIT

Every single step,
From the German's lonely cross
To where heaven and hill were lost
In black embrace
We paced the night:
Every
Single
Step.

Miles of precision,
Upwards, stepping,
Drowning in the atmosphere;
Why come from there to here?
Madmen!
Pilgrims,
Found belief
As dawn lifts out of the darkness' sheath
And Africa lies beneath.

That mad hallucination!;
Where the girls see lines of little men,
And the Englishman has a stroke,
Mafala has a smoke;
Red,
Forever.
And my swollen head is choked,
Spinning in the yoke of golden glaciers:
A carousel of angels
Takes my breath,
And I am resurrected
To what's left.

Seraphim and the Sunbird.

Green Malachite
And Red
The Sunbird sips
The flower,goldening.
Perfect lip
Perfect wing.

Seraphim's head
Is full of baggage.

Changing every day
Wearing him away;
Whilst beetles
Roll the world away,
Perfect work
Perfect play.

JAYZAY

Afterwards
In the Spring
I found a letter
From Zachariah.

John Zachariah
Has no boots.

Only his black skin
To walk a living
Out of the Earth.

He begs
That This Mother
Should not wear him down
That my shoes
Should come between them.

TANZANIA.

I can take the oils
From out of the earth.
Yes Master.

I can fly
And can journey under the sea.
Yes Master.

I gave you metal hands
To work the earth
And showed you how
To soothe the plagues you bear.
Yes Master.

And you have brought me
Nothing in your time.

Master No.
For I am your memory
I am the Time
When you and all the earth
Were One.

PURPLE MAN

Purple man
On the red earth
Striding mile after mile
Into the same day
As yesterday.

Masai Man
Hand on spear
Hand on Hand of Time
Holding each sunrise
To a second:

Holding the moon
On his silver brow
Keep time with God,
Letting the paler man
Go by.

Titles available from Pretani Press